OTHER PUFFIN BOOKS
YOU MAY ENJOY

Mary on Horseback

ROSEMARY WELLS

Mary on Horseback
Three Mountain Stories

PICTURES BY PETER McCARTY

PUFFIN BOOKS

To Mimi Donius

PUFFIN BOOKS
Published by the Penguin Group
Penguin Putnam Books for Young Readers,
345 Hudson Street, New York, New York 10014, U.S.A.
Penguin Books Ltd, 27 Wrights Lane, London W8 5TZ, England
Penguin Books Australia Ltd, Ringwood, Victoria, Australia
Penguin Books Canada Ltd, 10 Alcorn Avenue, Toronto, Ontario, Canada M4V 3B
Penguin Books (N.Z.) Ltd, 182-190 Wairau Road, Auckland 10, New Zealand

Penguin Books Ltd, Registered Offices: Harmondsworth, Middlesex, England

First published in the United States of America by Dial Books for Young Readers,
a division of Penguin Putnam Inc., 1998
Published by Puffin Books,
a division of Penguin Putnam Books for Young Readers, 2000

9 10

Text copyright © Rosemary Wells, 1998
Illustrations copyright © Peter McCarty, 1998
All rights reserved

THE LIBRARY OF CONGRESS HAS CATALOGED THE DIAL EDITION AS FOLLOWS:
Wells, Rosemary.
Mary on horseback: three mountain stories. / Rosemary Wells;
pictures by Peter McCarty.
p. cm.
Summary: Tells the stories of three families who were helped by the work of Mary
Breckinridge, the first nurse to go into the Appalachian Mountains and give medica
care to the isolated inhabitants. Includes an afterword with facts about
Breckinridge and the Frontier Nursing Service she founded.
ISBN 0-8037-2154-4 (tr.)—ISBN 0-8037-2155-2 (lib.)
1. Breckinridge, Mary, 1881–1965—Juvenile literature. 2. Nurses—Kentucky—
Juvenile literature. 3. Medical care—Kentucky—History—Juvenile literature.
4. Frontier Nursing Service, Inc.—Juvenile literature.
[1. Breckinridge, Mary, 1881–1965.
2. Nurses. 3. Women—Biography. 4. Frontier Nursing Service, Inc.] I. Title.
RT37.B72W44 1998 610.73'092—dc21 [B] 97-43409 CIP AC

Puffin Books ISBN 0-14-130815-X

Illustrations are based on photographs taken for the Frontier Nursing Service by
Marvin Breckinridge Patterson, used with permission of Marvin Breckinridge
Patterson. Photograph of Mary Breckinridge taken by Marvin Breckinridge Patterso
for the Frontier Nursing Service. Reproduced with permission of
Marvin Breckinridge Patterson.

Printed in the United States of America

CONTENTS

KENTUCKY 1923

IN 1923, AMERICANS DRIVE CARS, talk on the telephone, and use electric toasters. Planes fly overhead and people dance to jazz on the radio.

But in the Appalachian Mountains of Kentucky the twentieth century has not started. People live in tiny cabins without running water. They travel by mule on winding tracks and secret mountain pathways. They eke out hardscrabble livings by farming a little and hunting a little and moonshining, which is against the law. There are no radios. In the evening, fiddle music sings through the trees.

The Kentucky mountains are rich with devil's paintbrush and redbud. Before sunrise the valleys fill with clouds. After dark the hollows echo with a chorus of night creatures. . . . But beyond the wildflowers and the sound of the fiddle music, there is much suffering.

On a mountainside a little girl in a one-room cabin has third-degree burns from tending her mother's cooking fire. There is no hospital for over eighty miles and no car to take her there, or even a road to drive on.

In another valley a mother has just died giving birth to a stillborn baby. She leaves six other children. A nurse-midwife could have saved the mother and the baby, but there are no nurses here.

Over the river a boy of six has awakened with a fever of 105°. An inoculation will save his life, but there is no doctor to give it. Instead his father has gone to fetch the "granny woman," who will treat him with blackened pennies and leeches.

ON A SUMMER MORNING IN 1923 a woman comes riding into these mountains. Her name is Mary Breckinridge. She is a nurse. She will spend months here, treating fevers and binding wounds wherever she can. She will listen to the people. They tell her their troubles in an old-fashioned English much like the language their ancestors spoke in Scotland two hundred years before.

In her is a fiery will. She wants babies to be born healthy, and their mothers to live long lives. She intends to build a hospital here and to stop the typhoid, diphtheria, smallpox, and scarlet fever with a brigade of nurses on horseback.

She knows she needs more training to do this right and she must have help. But she will be back soon. In the years to come, her Frontier Nursing Service will save thousands of lives.

Here are three stories of people whose entire existence was changed by Mary Breckinridge.

~✦~

MOUNTAIN
MEDICINE

~✦~

WHEN MAMMA SEES FOUR MEN carrying Pa
home with his leg crushed, she screams.
The men try to make Mamma sit down. One of
them tells me, "There's a horse doctor with a bone
saw down in Krypton. We'll send him up to take
the leg off."

Mamma makes me fetch Biddy, the granny woman who takes care of our mountain people.

Biddy is over a hundred years old but she can
still rip the bark off a whole willow tree. She boils
the willow bark until it softens up like collard

greens. She cools it and packs it over Pa's leg. Then she puts an ax, blade up, under the bed to cut the fever. She leaves Mamma a folded paper of easing powder and goes away down the hollow to somebody else.

The easing powder doesn't do a speck of good, so Mamma gives Pa drops of turpentine against blood poisoning, and sips of white lightning against the pain.

"They're going to take his leg off, John," Mamma tells me. "Pa is never going to work again, and we have only those dimes in the mason jar."

If Pa can't work, we will have to move in with Mamma's sister Sally and Jip Cox. I'll have to sleep three to a bed with my big cousin Judah Cox and the baby. Supper time means eating their leftovers.

"Wait until the doctor comes," I say. "Wait until he comes." But both of us know the doctor got his license by sending away five dollars and a matchbook cover.

We wait a night and a day and another night and a day. Then I hear someone. A horse coming up Beech Fork makes a rushing noise in the deep gravel along the water's edge.

"Doctor's here!" I tell Mamma. But it isn't the doctor at all. It is a lady. She rides up the steep riverbank, shirtfront moon-white against our blue mountain evening.

When she comes to our door, a line of bats skims over her head but she doesn't pay them any mind, so I know she isn't a mincy city lady.

Right off she asks me my name, and I tell her it's John Hawkins.

"Well, my name is Mary Breckinridge. I'm a nurse," she says back.

Her voice has a softness to it. She takes off her jacket, and hangs it on a towel hook. Then she goes to Pa.

Shivers of bone show through Pa's leg. I can't look longer than an eye blink.

"How did this happen?" she asks.

But Mamma can't answer.

"I need you to help me," Mary tells my ma. "We're going to try and save this leg. We have to clean it up and splint it, and then in the morning we'll get him down the mountain to a hospital."

I run to the cool darkness of the woodshed to tend Mary's horse. That way I don't have to hear my pa cry out, or smell those nursey smells from what's inside Mary's saddlebags.

But I can't keep away. I go back and peek in the window of the cabin. Mary is holding a needle up to the light of the oil lamp. The silvery gleam of the point gives me the all-overs. She jabs it into a rubber-lidded bottle, then *spang* into Pa's arm.

I fall away from the window, sick as if I had soap suds in my belly. Bats circle me like swimming black handkerchiefs. I breathe in the smell of horse sweat and young corn until I get steady.

When I get back into the cabin, my mamma and my pa are both asleep. On the table I see Mary's saddlebags stuffed with evil-looking scissors and bottles.

"You've got your eye on that needle, haven't you, John?" Mary asks me, her blue eyes on my every move and a smile kicking at the corners of her mouth. She brings out sandwiches and offers me one. I have never tasted anything like chicken salad.

I wake up when voices and sunlight fill the house.

After breakfast Mary asks me, "How did your pa get hurt, John?"

"Ridin' the tides," I say.

"Tides?" says Mary. "Tell me what that means."

"Well," I say, "you know in the winter there's timber-cutting teams? They clear cut the big trees on the top of the mountain. Then the river men ride the logs down the chutes."

"Chutes?" asks Mary.

"Yes, ma'am. Chutes is where the water froths up mean and wild. Tides is when the water's real high and floody in the springtime. A river man rides a tree all the way from the top to the bottom of the mountain two days without stoppin'. My pa's a river man. He's good. The lumber company pays him extra. He didn't expect no accidents."

"No one ever does," says Mary.

From up the mountain Jip Cox and his brothers come to help. Two broom handles are run through the sleeves of two old coats and this makes a stretcher for Pa. My mamma's sister Sally is right behind the men, telling them what to do. No matter how I beg, Mamma won't let me go with them.

Four men carry the stretcher ends. They walk herky-jerky, trying not to jiggle Pa, and disappear into the shadows of a deer path alongside of Beech Fork. Pa's face is the color of a tallow candle.

I slip away after them, telling only Sister Sally, who has stayed to keep Mamma company. Sister Sally tries grabbing me by the wrist. "No, you don't go nowhere, John Hawkins!" she says. "Not nowhere!" But Sister doesn't want to spill the pail of shuck beans in her lap, and I am too quick for her.

I follow them down like a fox, stepping on no twigs, making no sound.

I don't show myself until noon when I get hungry. "Too late to send me back, ain't it?" I say.

Only Mary smiles. She pulls me up on her horse.

"I thought you might would give me a lickin'," I tell her.

"Once I had a little boy like you," says Mary. "I never was angry at him."

"What happened to him?" I ask her.

"I have no doubt he is sitting in God's lap in heaven this very minute, looking right down on us," she tells me.

We cross into Middle Fork. "Did you leave a note telling your mamma where you are, so she doesn't worry about you?" Mary asks.

"I told Sister Sally," I answer.

"Can you read and write, John?" asks Mary.

"No, ma'am," I answer. "Not a bit."

I feel Mary sigh in and out behind me. "How much does the lumber company pay a man for riding a fifty-foot tree trunk down a raging river for two days?" she asks me.

"Real good. Six dollars, Pa says."

Mary takes my hands. "Count out six fingers," she says.

But I only can do two and five. I hang my head.

Her arm circles me like Mamma's when I get a bee sting. Down the mountain we go. All the time I feel her arm around me.

"John," she says, "what are you going to be when you grow up?"

"River man like my pa," I say proudly.

I am afraid she'll say back, *Oh, why do you want to get crushed in the river?* She doesn't. She says, "You can be anything you want to be and so can I."

"But . . . but you already are," I say back.

"Not yet," says Mary.

"Well, what then are you going to be more?" I ask.

I feel her thinking behind me.

Then she says, "I've been riding all over this mountain country, John. Everybody here is very poor. But poor as they are, they share their bread with me and give me a place to sleep as if I were their own kin. Many of them need help. I intend to bring doctors and nurses and good medicine to the mountain people. I intend to build a hospital here if I have to brick and mortar it with my own hands."

Then she doesn't say more. But hearing her I feel the same as I did the night I sat on my pa's lap and we watched a shooting star from beginning to end across the sky.

AT THE BOTTOM OF THE MOUNTAIN Pa is taken to the Hyden Railway Station in a mule cart. He is bound for the hospital in Lexington. When he says good-bye, I kiss his face and hands. He is as hot as a chimney. We go back to Mary's big house at Wendover.

I don't ask after Pa for days on end. Quiet as a mouse I hoe weeds in the Wendover garden and collect eggs every morning. Will they fix my pa's leg? Will we have to live with Sister Sally? Big Judah haunts my sleep.

Miss Peacock and Miss Texas are Mary's other nurses. They feed me wonderful victuals. But Nurse Peacock sees me pick at my supper when I worry at night.

"John," says she one day, "the doctor sent word to say your pa's doing fine. Says he's going to keep his leg."

Big Judah goes on home from my dreams.

In the library Nurse Texas shows me how to write my name and read some out of a book. Nurse Peacock teaches me the dominos and I learn to count up all the numbers.

One evening Mary draws some careful squares on paper at the card table.

"What is that?" I ask.

"It's my plan for an outpost clinic at Beech Fork," she answers. She shows me how the lines on paper really mean rooms with doors and windows. She shows me how twelve inches make a foot. She tells me the clinic will be thirty feet by thirty feet. "There's a closet right here," she explains. "There's a kitchen and a sterilizer and a refrigerator. There's a waiting room for patients and a dispensary, where the nurses give out medicine. Morning sunshine comes in all the windows."

Mary gives me the ruler to keep. I study her

plan. I put Mary's picture of it, number by number, line by line, into my head.

In August Pa comes back from Lexington walking on both legs. Mary takes us to Camp Creek where Jip Cox and two mules meet us. My pa is not a good talker to women. Staring at the ground, he thanks Mary while he turns his hat in his hands.

I can see Mary in the eye of my memory. She eases out her reins and lets her horse eat from a patch of weeds. "Someday," she says, "I will need your help."

When I get home, I choose a flat pasture above Beech Fork. I collect up a barrelful of white stones. Then I lay out the plan for Mary's clinic, placing her ruler end over end in the grass. Thirty feet by thirty feet. Kitchen, waiting room, dispensary. My stones are large as goose eggs. They wait for her in the cornflowers, measured out just right for when she comes to build here.

If you were a hawk flying over, you could see them from the air.

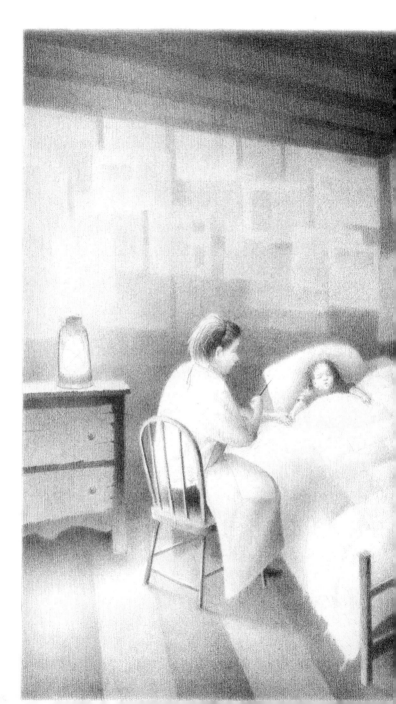

❧

IRELAND OF
SCOTLAND

❧

The Glasgow Times
APRIL 7, 1925

ATTENTION! NURSE GRADUATES
with a sense of adventure! Your own
horse, your own dog, and a thousand
miles of Kentucky mountains to serve.
Join my nurses' brigade and help save
children's lives. Write to:

M. BRECKINRIDGE
Hyden, Kentucky, U.S.A.

BEGIN MY LETTER TO KENTUCKY for the twentieth time.

To M. Breckinridge:

I am Margaret Ireland, registered nurse, eighteen and a half years old. I am on staff of St. Joseph's Hospital in Glasgow, Scotland, and wish to change my whole life because

And there my letter stops. I pencil in:

six days a week I put on a starched uniform and stand next to the ward surgeon with my hands at my sides like a parlor maid. I must never ask why he or the Sister Superior order anything. That's called giving cheek and I could lose my job.

I scratch this out. Instead I put in:

I love children. I am not afraid of hard work. I want to make my own path instead of slotting in to the way everybody else does things here in Glasgow.

Mum and Dad call up the stairway that we will be late for church. I seal the envelope, cover it with halfpenny stamps, and post it before I can snatch it back.

ON JUNE 24, 1925, I am four thousand miles from home at the last stop on the Louisville and Nashville Railroad. Quickly I put on red lipstick to look as old as I can.

M. Breckinridge is there to collect me. She has brought me a horse and riding pants.

"I'm Mary Breckinridge," she says. Her eyes are star blue and smiling. "This horse's name is Rick. He's yours. Ever been riding in the mountains?"

"I've never set foot off the pavements of Glasgow," I answer.

Mary grabs my left foot, locks it into the stirrup, and quick shoves my bottom onto the back of the horse. Off we go. I am so scared of falling off Rick that I sit pinned in the saddle like a bronze statue. A pine branch sticks out from nowhere. It smacks me off the horse. Mary has to dismount and help me back on again.

"Next time duck!" says Mary.

The horses swim right through a river that roars by like Noah's flood. I can't swim any better than I can ride, so I close my eyes and pretend none of this is happening.

"This is Thousandsticks Mountain," says Mary when we can hear one another again. "No one knows how many cabins are up here, but the children are dying of diphtheria, typhoid, scarlet fever, and smallpox. Right now diphtheria is the worst."

I look up between my horse's ears. I cannot see a single cabin or tell where one mountain begins and another ends.

Mary goes on, "Diphtheria vaccine is as expensive as liquid gold. We have just enough for sick children and their families. But we need to inoculate everyone. Your job is to count every man, woman, and child in these mountains."

"Count them?"

"The state of Kentucky has promised us serum for everyone if we turn in a list of the families by September." Mary leans back in her saddle. "I want to be ready to set up an inoculation clinic for the whole county on October first. Of course, as you go, you must treat everyone who needs you. It's quite a job, Miss Ireland of Scotland!"

When I get off the horse at Wendover, I don't think I'll walk or sit for a week. Nurse Texas and Nurse Peacock introduce me to all the dogs and horses.

"Will you be coming out in the mountains with me?" I ask them shyly.

"Oh, no!" they answer. "Until we get more nurses, there's just Mary and us for the whole county. One of us must always be on call here. The other goes twenty miles down to Beech Fork. Mary's building an outpost clinic there."

Over my first breakfast at Wendover Mary says, "Maggie, I'll take you up the mountain myself until you learn the ropes. After that you're on your own."

I follow her, flopping in my saddle like Raggedy Ann. Along every path Mary points out wasp nests, certain stony river-bends, and mossy tree-stumps.

"Remember these," she says. "It's how you find your way back."

Mountain children watch us like owls as we pick our way up the paths to their cabins. Some have fleas and sores on their faces. Some wear shirts that are too small, some are bare from the waist down.

We have begun to count families. I keep the list in my nurse's daybook. We knock on the door of every cabin we find. There is always a child who needs our help. The mothers watch Mary's every move as she treats infected eyes and burned fingers. They look right through me.

One mother asks me, "How old do you be?" as she brushes molasses onto biscuit dough.

I blush. "Nineteen," I answer smartly. I want to tell this woman to clean her kitchen table. To feed her children greens or they'll get scurvy. To brush their teeth, for the love of God! I bite hard on my thoughts and swallow them whole.

Later I complain to Mary, "They won't let me near them!"

Mary tells me, "You must never show annoy-ance with anybody, Maggie. They will think you are putting on airs."

On my eighth morning at Wendover a boy comes to the house and asks for Miz Breckinridge. His name is John Hawkins and he's been sent by a sick child's mother far up beyond Devil's Gap. Mary has left in the middle of the night to attend the birth of a baby. Suddenly it is time for me to go into the mountains on my own.

I saddle Rick and follow John. How will I ever find my way back down? John shows me twelve trees on a mountain ridge. "This is where we cross the stream," he says.

After about four hours John stops and points. "This here's the fork to my home," he says to me. "T'other way is Devil's Gap. Keep on. You're bound to find a real shackly cabin with a mean-eyed goat and a she-balsam tree in the front yard. Their name's Gibbs."

I almost give up. Then I find the goat tied out-side a half-collapsed cabin. Star Gibbs is four years

old and has a fever of 105°. Her mother has been
up with her all night. "Sure enough it's milk poisoning," says Star's mother.

It is diphtheria. "She needs an injection," I say,
"or we will lose her."

"My man don't hold with needles," she says, "so
I'll turn my back."

I give Star an ounce of our precious serum. Four
pair of eyes watch me from the window. Then they
disappear. The walls of this cabin are steeped in
fever. Soon the whole family will be sick unless I
inoculate them. I ask the children to come for their
shots, but they scatter off.

While her mother rests, Star lies in my lap. I
wish I could give her ice cream as I would in Glasgow. But here there are no refrigerators and no ice
cream, so I tell her about them and name the fla-
vors while her fever eases. Chocolate, vanilla, and
pistachio.

An older sister creeps onto the porch and lis-
tens. "My name is Lavender," she tells me, and
shows me her doll. It is a shred of rag glued to a

stone head. A smile and two eyes are painted on the stone.

At sunset the children's father comes home. Their mother mixes old coffee with hot bacon grease and pours it over biscuits and fatback. We crowd around the fly-specked table in the cabin's single room. I sit facing a wall lined with stained newspaper. The father thanks God for his family and the fatback with red-eye gravy.

When I have finished eating, I sit as straight as I can. "Excuse me," I say. "After supper you must let me give you the same medicine that Star had so that you don't get sick too. It's only a wee jab and it won't hurt a bit."

A dead silence greets the word "jab." I beg the father to be first. He grins. Half his teeth are missing. "Pretty young thing like you ain't stickin' no needles in my tough old hide!" he answers.

Everyone laughs. I have lost again.

The children sleep five to a bed. I lie down on a blanket on the floor. Someone kneels next to me in the darkness, staring. "Tell again, Nursie," whispers Lavender. "Tell over again about the ice creams."

In the morning Star is better, and I can leave. Her mother gives me a chicken gizzard sandwich for my saddlebag. Lavender is all bright-eyed and smiley, cheeks warm from the sun. She holds her stone doll up for a kiss good-bye.

I keep the stream on my left and follow it down the mountain in the mist. Nothing looks familiar. While I search for the mossy stump by the third beech tree, something ugly prickles my mind. I brush it away and think about finding a path to Wendover. It takes me the whole day.

OVER SUPPER I STARE into the flame of the oil lamp.

"Tell me," says Mary. "Tell me what happened."

"No one lets me near them with a needle," I say. "I am a failure. I might as well go home to Scotland for all the use I am."

"No, Maggie," says Mary. "You're still learning. October is a long way off."

I tell Mary about Lavender's stone doll. In my mind's eye Lavender says good-bye. Her eyes are so bright. Her cheeks so sun-warm.

At the supper table I sit bolt upright. It had been a misty morning. Lavender's bright eyes were dilated with fever not sun. Any nurse trainee could have seen that.

"I must go back up!" My voice is shaking. "She could be dead by morning."

Mary sips her coffee. The light of the oil lamp swims in her eyes. "If you were a failure, Maggie, you wouldn't hear that child calling you," she says softly.

Rick does not like a night journey. In the moonlight a possum crosses our path and spits at us. Rick balks. I gather up my reins and kick him on. I remember to keep the stream on my right. Against the dawn sky I find the twelve trees on the mountain ridge. At seven I find the cabin almost hidden in a patch of cloud.

Lavender is lying white and still on her corncob mattress. Her mother wants me to give her the serum that saved Star's life. Her father wants me to give her whiskey and easing powder as if I were a granny woman. I tell him no. He storms around the cabin. "I wouldn't let the good Lord himself stick me with one of them pokers. Not for nothin' nohow!" he says.

Suddenly Lavender's mother stands up and shouts, "You're a yellow-bellied coward, Enos Gibbs! 'Fraid to have a needle your ownself. Look at this beautiful, educated young lady come all the way just for our Lavender. You think you can outsharp her? Look at that gold nurse badge on her. You think they give those out to nobody?"

Lavender comes around slowly. We whisper the names of the ice creams, eating them in our minds. I tell her about telephones and the ocean between here and my home.

THAT AFTERNOON I WRITE in my nurse's day-book: *July 3, 1925, 3 p.m. Gibbs family, Diph. Inoc. complete.* Then I visit the next cabin and the next, all the way down the mountain.

I count the last family by mid-September. The state of Kentucky sends us a wagon-load of vaccine. On October 1, 1925, the Beech Fork outpost clinic is completed. Our first day is spent inoculating all the children from a nearby one-room schoolhouse.

Neither the children nor their teacher has ever seen an electric lightbulb or heard a radio. Thanks to our modern three-kilowatt generator, we have both. Mary and I string five electric bulbs over our worktable. The radio picks up a signal from West Virginia. The sun vanishes and the autumn evening falls quickly.

The children love the lightbulbs and touch them shyly. They love the sound of the Betty Bumpis Band singing all the way from Charleston. But they freeze when they see the hypodermics on the table.

"Needles are sheerly the work of the devil," says their teacher.

I am furious at the teacher, but I say nothing. Mary snaps off the lights and the radio and says to the teacher, "The children will do as you do. Without these shots you will lose half of them. Have you thought of that? Are you going to show your children cowardice or spunk?"

The children wiggle in their thin dresses and frayed trousers. The teacher hangs her head. She is no match for Mary Breckinridge, and she knows it.

"Have I got one brave boy or girl who'll volunteer to be first to be injected?" Mary asks.

No one answers.

"Come along, now! Who'll be first?" I say.

No answer. Then one little voice pipes up. It is Lavender. "I had a shot this summer!" she says. "And my little sister Star too. They don't hurt more than a pinprick."

A flax-haired boy rolls up his sleeve. The rest line up, one by one behind him.

We snap the lights and radio back on, and a hundred years of darkness flee away. Into the mountain night floats the music of another world. A far-off orchestra plays "I Once Had a Wonderful Dream." The children sway and follow the melody's sweetness.

When we are finished, I take Lavender into the clinic's brand-new kitchen.

"There's a little white house with a door!" says Lavender.

"It's a refrigerator," I tell her. "Open it up, now."

The freezer has only room for one Dixie Cup. It is half chocolate, half vanilla. Lavender eats every bite as if it came straight from heaven. The radio plays "Make Believe the Moon Is Made of Silver."

"I am making believe," says Lavender.

~∽~

HOW MANY STARS
IN MY CROWN?

~∽~

THE TWINS WERE BORN MAY 4, 1932. Mamma went down with childbed fever soon after. Pa got her the preacher. The preacher said he intended to breathe the breath of the Lord into her lungs because of the two little babies needin' their mamma. That left me entirely out of the picture, but it wasn't any use to say, "What about me?" Mamma was too far gone for the breath of the Lord.

I patted her hot hand, and I said over and over, "Mamma, don't leave me. Don't die. Can you hear me? It's your ownliest sugarplum talking. It's Pearl. Can you hear me?"

The preacher told me to sit quiet and not to get in the Lord's way. Just before Mamma left this earth on her way to heaven, I felt all her last strength drain into my hand. Then her spirit went on up through the open window into the night. I watched out the window and thought I saw her move across the sky and say good-bye, but I'm not sure it wasn't a cloud.

I looked up when the preacher was gone, and my pa was in the corner of the room in the dark. That's where we stayed with Mamma until morning. Since then I have not spoken a single word.

The twins hardly ate after Mamma died. My pa'll be the first to tell you he doesn't know one thing about babies. He wanted to lean on me to keep the twins alive. He couldn't do that, and he knew it.

So Pa drank three cups of coffee in a row and told me the twins were going to die if we didn't get them down to that new hospital at Hyden. That's more than a two-day ride straight downhill.

Pa said, "I'm clean out of cash money. Not a red cent, so we'll take the cow for payment."

We made our way down the mountain along Hell-fer-Sartin Creek—Pa in the saddle holding Eva, and me on the mule's rump holding Ben. Those babies didn't even cry anymore. At night Pa built a fire and we warmed the twins up. I milked the cow and soaked the corner of a handkerchief in the milk. I tried to get them to suck on it, but they wouldn't take but a dib.

We wrapped them together like two little hurt sparrows in their blanket. They were still breathing in and out, but that's about all.

Late the next morning we came to the hospital. Pa didn't say a word, he just handed Eva over to a nurse. She took Ben too.

"Keep the cow please, ma'am, in payment," said Pa. I was holding the cow's rope. "This here's Pearl. I want her to stay on and learn how to raise up these babies. Pearl is a real good girl and will earn her keep. She ain't said a word since her mamma died, but she ought to come around soon."

Pa gave me a little smile. "I'll fetch you home by first frost."

Pa turned the mule's head up the path and clucked to her to get on.

"Won't you speak, little girl? What's your name?" the nurses asked me. I shook my head and did not answer their questions, so they stopped asking. All the same, I liked those nurses in their blue coats. I could not keep my eyes off them. They moved like beautiful angels from the Garden of Paradise.

Each morning I sat on the steps of the hospital and watched every little thing going on. I picked wildflowers and made daisy chains and crowns of butter and eggs. The third morning a lady wheeled herself up in a wheelchair. "My name is Mary Breckinridge," she said. "I'm pleased to meet you."

I didn't answer.

"Nurse Texas told me about you, Pearl. You lost your mother. Is that right?"

No answer from me, but here was the first person on earth who knew I lost Mamma as well as Eva and Ben losing her. Right then I almost told Mary Breckinridge what would happen if I even spoke one word. I might cry forever and ever. I didn't want to do that kind of crying.

I followed her into the building. "Here I am in this wheelchair because I broke my back falling off a horse. After eight years in the saddle riding in these mountains—can you imagine that?" she asked. "But I'll be on my feet in no time. Meanwhile you can help me. I've got six hospital clinics, twenty-two nurses, and five couriers to direct and take care of and pay for and see it all works perfectly. How about that?"

She had a pile of mail as big as the post office at Hell-fer-Sartin. She let me lick the stamps for her envelopes. "Pearl," she said, "you don't have to say a blessed word if you don't want to. Too many people talk my ear off anyway."

In my lap was a daisy chain.

"Put that lovely flower garland around my neck, Pearl," said Mary Breckinridge. "It'll cheer up my whole day." She gave me more stamps to lick and set me sorting paper clips and elastic bands. I got 'em all in straight lines for her.

Next morning I waited for Mary again. I made

her a crown of buttercups and wild roses. She put it right on her head. "Now I'm the Queen of the Wheelchair Brigade, Pearl," she said, and we were back at work.

"You've never seen a telephone, have you, child?" said Mary.

I shook my head. I watched her talk on it. Was she talking to the wind?

I eat with the nurses. Because I don't speak, they talk in front of me as if I am deaf too. I hear about Ben and Eva. It will be Christmas before they can go home, said one. Holding their own all the same, said another. In the evenings Nurse Peacock and Nurse Ireland play cards with me, double solitaire and hearts. They bet pennies on gin rummy, and they let me use bottle caps.

I sleep upstairs in the children's ward. Mostly it's quiet, but one night I heard Mary's wheelchair. Then I heard screams. I crept down the corridor and watched. The nurses were caring for a little girl. I could hardly look at her. She burned all over.

The next morning Mary told me to give my buttercup necklace to the little burned girl, Lily. I put it right where she could see it. Two eyes peered out of the bandages, blinked at the flowers, and looked at me.

After three days Lily said something. I couldn't understand because of the bandages across her mouth. She said it again. It was water she wanted. I put a glass straw through her lips.

I could not talk to Lily, but I could hum. "How Many Stars Will There Be in My Crown?" That's my favorite song. Then I brought out a deck of cards and dealt out hearts, me playing for both of us. Her feet were unburned and I bathed them in cool water. I combed what there was of her hair. She liked it. I could tell.

After six days Lily's bed was suddenly empty. I looked everywhere for her. Finally I went into Mary's office.

"Lily has died, Pearl," Mary said. She watched me carefully. I made only little sounds like a kitten mewing. The clock ticked away time until Mary took out a shoe box full of photographs of children. She set them out on her desk like solitaire cards.

"Come and look, Pearl," she said, and picked up two of the pictures.

"This is my son, Breckie, and my daughter, Polly, when she was just born. They both died when they were so young. For a while I wanted to follow them to heaven. But instead I studied to be a nurse."

Mary fanned out the rest of the pictures. "After the Great War they sent us American nurses to France because thousands of children needed help. The boys and girls in these pictures are the ones we saved. I know each one by name."

I edged over to Mary's shoulder and we looked at all the pictures and she read out the funny snurled-up names from that far-off land of France.

We listened to the clock again for a while. Then we put away the pictures. "There's not much the doctor could do for Lily. I've seen a dozen little girls burned because their dresses catch fire from the cooking stoves. Little boys are safer. They wear overalls."

Mary typed out a letter. I couldn't read it, but she told me what it said. It was to a factory asking them to give us a couple of crates of children's overalls for her to pass out to mountain families so there'll be no more little girls on fire.

I put on the stamp nice and straight.

One day Mary left. She was going to Lexington, she said, to have her back brace taken off so she could ride again. "Hold the fort, Pearl," Mary said.

She was gone a whole week. I rolled pennies and cleaned out every single letter of her typewriter keys with Bon Ami on a toothbrush. I sharpened the pencils and sorted the little hickies in the china dish over the mantel.

Mary came home walking. The wheelchair was gone. She brought with her two big boxes. In them were a hundred pair of overalls all little sizes. Every nurse got some to hand out.

At first Mary could only ride for a little bit, but at the end of the summer she said, "I'm good as store-bought now, Pearl. Are you coming with me?"

I got a donkey called Coolidge. We went up Hurricane Creek where there's lots of cabins. At each one Mary said, "Good afternoon, ma'am. I'm from the Frontier Nursing Service. Do you have a little girl and does she tend the cooking fire for you?" Mary went into every cabin while I held her horse and Coolidge.

At the last cabin of the day Mary saw a little girl. "Size four, Pearl," she said. "I'm too sore and tired to get off and on another time. Square up your shoulders, hold your head high, and speak out!"

I didn't even think to refuse Mary.

"Good afternoon, ma'am," said I at the cabin door. "I'm from the Frontier Nurses. Does your little girl yonder tend your cooking fire?"

We went home along the creek-bed in the twilight. Me on my donkey, Mary on horseback.

✍ MARY BRECKINRIDGE ✎

MARY BRECKINRIDGE'S LIFE is not a story of rags to riches. Much rarer, hers is a passage from aterial riches to riches of the spirit.

She was born in 1881 and grew up in a large and ving family. The Breckinridges were among the ost distinguished names of the Old South. Mary's andfather, Confederate General John C. Breckinridge, rved as vice-president of the United States under mes Buchanan. Her father was the American minis-r to Russia.

Eight-year-old Mary learned to ride in the hills of entucky. She learned to speak French fluently at a viss boarding school and even lived in Russia. She me and went easily among America's most influen-il and privileged families.

Like any other wealthy young woman of her time, ary might simply have married and decorated some an's life and career. This was not to be. Her young husband died. She married again and had two children. Both children died and she lost her second husband as well. She fell beyond mourning into despair.

All the grief and passion that was in her at that moment in time came out in her decision to become a nurse so that other children might have a chance to live. She enrolled in St. Luke's Hospital School of Nursing in New York City in 1907.

After the First World War Mary went to France as part of the American nurses' corps. The beautiful French farmlands were an ocean of mud, blasted towns, and broken families. Mary describes seeing children crying with hunger at the same time that cows, their udders painfully full, were crying to be milked. Mary Breckinridge and her fellow nurses helped at least ten thousand homeless and starving children, giving them food, life, and hope.

When Mary returned from France, she went to the Appalachian Mountains of Kentucky, where she knew that the people lived poorer lives than anywhere in America. In her mind were the stirrings of an idea which was to become the formation of the Frontier Nursing Service. Over the years it would be a model for rural nursing services worldwide. "If I could do it here, in Kentucky," she wrote, "no one could claim that their terrain was too difficult."

In 1925 there were three nurses working with Mary Breckinridge. By 1928 there were thirty. By 1931 Mary had overseen the building of six outpost clinics and a forty-bed hospital. In 1931 *Life* magazine ran a six-page picture essay on the nurses on horseback.

Since it was established, the FNS has registered two hundred and fifty thousand patients and delivered twenty-five thousand healthy babies. Frontier Nurses now visit an average of thirty-five thousand mountain homes each year.

Mary Breckinridge's success drew visitors from every country. Presidents and princes, doctors and journalists visited her at Wendover. One doctor from India said of Mary Breckinridge, "She had in her the elegance of past ages, the graciousness of daily life, and the courage to ride a spacecraft."

On May 16, 1965, Mary Breckinridge died, her dream in this world complete—not because her work was finished, but because it would go on.

ACKNOWLEDGMENTS

I would like to thank the Frontier Nursing Service—particularly Barb Gibson—for its generous help. I would also like to thank the staff at the University of Kentucky, Lexington, and the Mary Breckinridge archives for sharing their knowledge with me. Marvin Breckinridge Patterson, Mary Breckinridge's niece and personal photographer, as well as her assistant, Priscilla Becker, have been extremely generous with their time, information, and photographs.

The characters in these three stories are true-to-life. They are based on Marvin Breckinridge's 1930 film, *The Forgotten Frontier,* and details from Mary Breckinridge's autobiography, *Wide Neighborhoods.*   —R.W.

When she read Mary Breckinridge's autobiography, **Rosemary Wells** was so struck by it that she went to Kentucky to learn more about Mary and the Frontier Nursing Service. After visiting Wendover, Mary Breckinridge's home, and talking with the nurses at the FNS, Mrs. Wells felt that Mary Breckinridge's story should be shared with today's young people. The result is *Mary on Horseback*.

Rosemary Wells is the author of more than fifty books, including the beloved picture and board books about Max and Ruby. She lives in Westchester County, New York.

Visit her website at **www.rosemarywells.com.**